Royal Air Force
1941 - 1945

A.R. TAYLOR D.F.C.

Pen Press Publishers Ltd

© A.R Taylor 2005

All rights reserved

No part of this publication may be reproduced,
stored in a retrieval system, or transmitted
in any form or by any means, without
the prior permission in writing of the publisher,
nor be otherwise circulated in any form of binding or cover
other than that in which it is published and without a similar
condition including this condition being imposed on the
subsequent purchaser.

First published in Great Britain by
Pen Press Publishers Ltd
39-41, North Road
Islington
London N7 9DP

ISBN 1-904754-76-7

Printed and bound in the UK

A catalogue record of this book is available from
the British Library

Cover design by Jacqueline Abromeit

War is always hateful. But if ever there was a conflict between good and evil then the Second World War was it. Emerging from our shared silence my German friend turned to me and said; "I hope you realise how lucky you are to know that your parents, and your country were on the right side."
Indeed I do.

WO1 A.R. TAYLOR 657376

The following is a record of my service in the RAF with excerpts from diaries which I kept at the time.

A copy of these papers is held in the RAF Museum, Hendon, and also in the Norwich Archives, as well as in the Imperial War Museum

RAF Stations

Map of Stations where I was posted

The Army

On 18.12.40, while reading Company Orders, I discovered that the RAF were looking for volunteers for aircrew. About 200 from my Battalion applied and our Colonel, who was understandably upset at the thought of losing so many trained men, pointed out that few of us were bright enough to be accepted. The number of applicants then dropped dramatically to 15.

The Battalion was stationed in Coleraine, Northern Ireland at the time, and on 3.4.41 we 15 were taken to Belfast by truck for our RAF examinations. We went first to the railway station where we had tea and buns at the Free Canteen which was run by a fat and cheerful woman who swore like a trooper and was very popular with the boys! After this we went to a house in the suburbs where we were individually asked questions about maths and general knowledge, and then another building nearby for a pretty stiff medical. At the end of the day only two of us, Fred Pym and myself, were accepted for training as Air Observers.

Some abbreviations in common use in the RAF

Binding	Studying
Bull's Eye	Bombing an infra-red beam at night
Ditch	To land in the sea
DR	Dead Reckoning Navigation
ETA	Expected Time of Arrival
Gardening	Mine laying
Happy Valley	The Ruhr
Heavies	4-Engined Bombers
Irvine	Fur-lined Jacket
Kite	Aeroplane
LAC	Leading Aircraftsman
LMF	Lacking moral fibre
Mae West	Inflatable Jacket
Ops	Operational flight over enemy territory.
OTU	Operational Training Unit
Port	Left
Prang	Crash (or "A Good Prang" to describe a successful attack on a target)
RT	Radio Telephone
Starboard	Right
U/s	Unserviceable
W/OP	Wireless Operator
Wimpey	Wellington Bomber

The RAF

I left the Battalion on 2.6.41 and arrived at Stratford-upon-Avon the following day, where I was billeted at the Arvon Hotel next door to a parish church. On 13.6.41 we all had a skin inspection on the stage of the Shakespeare Memorial Hall. We took our turn to file past the MO, cheered by our mates! That evening we went to this same hall for a fine performance of *Romeo and Juliet*.

I was posted to No.6 Initial Training Wing, Aberystwyth on 15.6.41 where we were split up into Wings and Squadrons and wore white flashes in our caps. I was billeted at the Royal Lion Hotel where I shared a room with Fred Pym and Cliff Street. Cliff and I became good friends and while on this course I helped him with his exams and taught him to swim in the sea.

Reveille was at 6 a.m., work finished at 6 p.m. and the course lasted six weeks; during which time we studied signals, armaments, gas, law, hygiene, aircraft recognition, maths and navigation. The weather was hot and we marched from one class to another at the astonishing speed of 150 paces per minute, which is as close to running as you can get. The infantry pace I was used to was 110 paces per minute – i.e. about 3 mph.

On 4.9.41 I was promoted to LAC and my pay went up to £3.16s a fortnight, of which £1.8s went to my mother.

Cliff and I were posted to Penrhos, North Wales, on 29.9.41 for flying training. We were billeted in a house in Llanbedrog, a village three miles from the aerodrome and close to the sea. Our daily routine was to get up at 6.30 a.m. when we were transported to the aerodrome. Work finished at 5 p.m. when we were driven back to our billets, where we had supper and studied till about 9 p.m. Mr Chatfield, our landlord, used to own a shop in London, but after it was bombed he and his wife decided to run this boarding house. He told us that the Government paid him 6d per head per night for our keep and it was difficult to know how he made ends meet.

On 21.10.41 I recorded in my diary "Binding like a swine. Spend a lot of time knocking MET into Cliff's head. Even the experts agree that no amount of knowledge of this subject is any good in this country. English weather seems to be against any such intimacy as forecasting."

On the night of 24.10.41 there was a blitz on Liverpool and we saw the flashes lighting up the sky over the hills.

Diary entry for 15.12.41:

Cliff and I were detailed for bombing and we accordingly went round the field to the dispersal hut. On arrival we were ordered to help the armourer fuse some bombs. Very well, we thought, we know all about this:
1. Clean the detonator sleeves, making sure… etc.
2. If there is any friction discard the bomb as being U/S… etc, etc.

However, the armourer had other ideas and rammed the deadly things into dirty sockets, occasionally whacking them in with a piece of wood. When Cliff pointed out the error of his ways the armourer looked up with a scornful eye, spat with precision and carried on. We gave him a cigarette and he condescended to speak to us. Later he helped us to bomb-up our kite. We had them up and the pins out and were carrying out the final test when we found that one of the units was out of order. We fiddled about for some time re-adjusting clamps, testing electric wires and the like but to no effect. So we turned to our armourer. His method was simple yet effective. He pulled the bomb off the rack, swung it back to his arm's length and smote the unit three times with a great clang. Quite casually he hung the bomb up again and was not in the least surprised to discover it now worked perfectly. Finally it rained and we didn't go up.

Christmas Day 1941 was grey and drizzly. After a few drinks at the local we went back to our boarding house for a lunch of duck and stuffing and a glass of sherry. We all laughed a lot and the children got excited and spilled water all over the table.

In January '42 we spent much time with a retired Merchant Navy officer studying the stars and practising Astro Navigation.

Finally we took a number of exams which included maps and charts, MET, compass and instruments, bombing, gunnery, wireless and navigation.

*

What follows relates to flying experiences from October '41 to August '42.

3.10.41

Went up this morning in an Anson, my first flight. Flew over the hills to Aberystwyth where we saw some of the lads drilling on the front, then up again to Colwyn Bay and down the coast to Penrhos. Very calm.

10.10.41

Up again this morning in an Anson. I found that if I took my eye off the map for five minutes I was lost. A grand day – terrific exhilaration looking down over miles of hills and valleys chequered with cloud shadows, and villages you could slip into your pocket.

Up again this evening towards Liverpool and then over Snowdon. Pretty cold at 3,000 feet.

18.10.41

Flying again today – am getting to know this part of Wales pretty well. For the first time flew over cloud at 6,000 feet and noticed what a detached feeling this gives you. Pretty calm and cold flying at that height.

Near the hills down low if there's any wind at all it's bumpy; the plane drops or jerks suddenly and then carries on as if nothing had happened.

11.11.41

A cold, grey day. Flying for the first time for a month and in a Blenheim for the first time. These planes were built for the Observer but he must have short legs, four eyes and a fantastic number of hands. Flew to Wrexham, Shrewsbury and Bala and it all went like clockwork.

20.11.41

We have missed the last flying days through rain and fog. However, today was fine and I went up with Misk on our first bombing run. We were to have dropped the bombs low level at Hell's Mouth. Misk was first on the bomb sight but the bombs refused to fall although we pressed every button in sight. One of the engines conked out as we were landing but we made it alright. The trouble with the bombing turned out to be that the electrical release switches were out of order – and we hadn't taken the pins out.

26.11.41

Lindsay packed up today. In one of his letters home he had said that he would never fly on Ops. This was intercepted by the censor and sent to the CO. Trouble is his missis doesn't even know he is in aircrew so he had no choice but to pack up. He use to be the manager of the Opera House in Belfast.

29.11.41

Cliff and I flying bombing this afternoon in a long-nosed Blenheim. Before we took off I made absolutely sure that all the pins were out.

Target Hell's Mouth again flying at four and eight hundred feet. There is nothing like it! I let out a primitive whoop of joy the first time the aircraft turned and I could see the little target almost hidden in the smoke from my bomb. Cliff too was one mass of delighted grins, turning around to us as each bomb burst and raising his thumb as if it was the real thing.

2.12.41

Since we arrived here six planes have landed with their undercarts up but luckily no one injured. But about a week ago a Blenheim crashed on the edge of the drome, killing No.2 navigator and injuring No.1 and the pilot.

4.12.41

Came second in the bombing. Jock, Nick and another lad failed but I'm glad to say they are still on the course.

It's marvellous how people curse this course, but tear their hair out in handfuls when thrown out.

26.12.41

A week ago a Blenheim stalled from a height and crashed on the bank that runs around the 'drome. All were killed including one of the navigators, Tebby, who only the day before had been telling us what he intended to do on his leave which was due to start the next day.

28.12.41

In Cliff's first DR trip the other day, owing to an error in calculating drift, he got 25 miles off track in two hours. Is this a record?

12.1.42
Flying all day with Cliff navigating. Went out over the Irish Sea almost to Wicklow Head, then to the Isle of Man and back to base before midday.

There have been a number of accidents recently. Last night an Anson ditched in the bay and the crew were out in the dinghy till ten this morning, a wickedly cold night. A Walrus brought them in. Then this morning another Anson headed into the sea with its six occupants who were all drowned. And this afternoon another Anson crashed into a mountain-side with two killed.

14.1.42
Got up for an hour this morning in a Boulton Paul Defiant and fired at a drogue, managing somehow to get the best score in the class. By revolving the turret at the same time that the plane turns, you get the distinct feeling that you are sailing away into space.

15.1.42
One of the coldest days I can remember. I was first navigator this morning in an Anson. Got very close to the Irish coast where visibility was bad and we then changed course for Ayre Point on the Isle of Man. A mist closed in on us and we could only dimly see white wavecaps directly below us. Got a wireless fix and on the strength of that steered for Great Ormes Head, arriving there smack on ETA much to the surprise of the pilot who was convinced that we were lost. I was pretty pleased with myself as we had been travelling for three hours over the sea in a strong wind and without sight of land. Did a further two hours flying this afternoon.

9.1.42
Cliff and I invented a drift-finding machine last night which, if it works, should be a great help to navigators.

(Note: This invention was later turned down by the Air Ministry.)

25.2.42

Flew as first navigator this morning and was dead-on the whole time. A glorious day but misty. The pilot, a Pole, got very impatient and dive-bombed practically everything in sight. We flew in and out of little bays above the mull of Galloway, the water very clear and green. Put the breeze up a village at one stage by flying between the masts of a ship at anchor.

22.3.42 – 10.4.42

Busy as hell the whole time flying till 8 and 9 at night.

One day there was a gale blowing and we got into an air pocket over the mountains and dropped 450 feet. Another day they split Cliff and I up to see if we could work independently, and we had to make a forced landing at Squires Gate, Blackpool, in driving rain.

During the last four days we have been doing a lot of high level bombing and I haven't been very successful so far. My teeth give me infernal trouble at height and make it damned hard for me to concentrate.

(Note: A clever RAF dentist later discovered that a minute pocket of air was trapped between a filling and a nerve. As air expands with height, he had found the cause for my toothache and was able to put it right.)

On completion of training at Penrhos I was awarded my beret and was promoted to sergeant.

9.5.42

Posted to Hinton where we are billeted in a Nissen but about two miles from the camp. We are flying in Ansons and doing only navigation.

Met my pilot in a bus returning from Oxford late one night. The meeting was quite accidental but when I discovered that he was looking for an Observer I teamed up with him. His name is Ernie and I can only describe him as being small and dark. We found the W/Op AG in the same casual way a few days later – name of Jason.

19.5.42
Today Nick and Stokes were in an Anson doing low flying. It was one of those bumpy tempestuous days, the sky full of racing and angry grey clouds. Their kite got into a pocket and dropped smack onto a ploughed field, but by some miracle the pilot managed to lift her nose up again and brought her back on one engine with both propellers bent right back at the tips.

21.5.42
The pilots are doing a conversion course learning to fly Blenheims and watched with keen interest by their crews. Ernie nearly crashed and Jason and I threatened him with the sack if he does it again!

24.5.42
Arrived at 13 OTU Bicester today.

25.5.42
Had an hour on the Link Trainer with Ernie this afternoon. Pretty tricky at first but was getting the hang of it by the time I finished.

26.5.42
Bombed from 6,000 ft. Warm and steady as a pond. Bicester afterwards where we drank beer and talked shop.

3.6.42
Bombing ended today. Came out with top score at height level which is pleasing.

4.6.42

Albert Wheeler killed today. Engines cut just after take-off.

9.6.42

Started OT (Operational Training) flight today where we test our skills at everything we have been taught. I must say we are bloody good as a crew and I feel as if we could go anywhere and do any damn thing. Never felt happier in a job in my life.

10.6.42 – 19.6.42

Most of this time was spent flying with a bit of ground instruction thrown in. One day we were practising map-reading around Maidenhead and after a few turns decided to return to base. The other kite in the formation got a little way from us and was hidden by low cloud. A few minutes later, looking back through the perspex, I saw its great dark shape sweep not five feet above our tail.

3.7.42

After some leave, went back to Bicester. All our training has had one object in view – close co-operation with the Army and shipping sweeps, but the situation in the Middle East is very uncertain at the moment and nothing has been done about our postings.

10.7.42

Learned this morning that we are being posted to Upwood on Sunday for night-flying training before going on to 2 Group. To us this means a posting to the Middle East flying Bostons. Jerry has had it now!

12.7.42

Our posting to Upwood has been cancelled and the crew is to go instead to Finningley in Yorkshire.

13.7.42

Spent all day in and out of trains, and we had two hours to spare in Sheffield. It was raining and I don't think I have ever seen anything quite as dismal. The smoke lay like a blanket over the town, everything was black with soot and scattered about lay wrecks of buildings gutted in the Blitz. Arrived at Finningley in the evening. The camp is about 12 miles from Doncaster and I am billeted in a room with Ernie, Jason and another observer nicknamed Tomo.

(Note: We flew Wellingtons at Finningley, Bircotes and Wing.)

14.7.42

Lecture by Station Adjutant this morning when he told us that we are to be trained to fly in Lancasters and that the Observers are to become bomb aimers. I must say I felt pretty sick when I heard this news as we had been doing so well as a three-man team in our twin-engined aircraft.

16.7.42

Have by now become resigned to what is going on. For one thing, if we are to be on heavies I would sooner be a bomb aimer than a navigator. I will at least be able to see what is going on. Jason has also had to give up one of his trades – from now on he will be a W/Op, pure and simple, and no longer a W/Op AG.

23.7.42

Air raid warning sounded tonight but nobody seemed to bother about it, and kites took off normally on their exercises, roaring over our billet on their way out.

24.7.42

Last night two of the kites, both without lights owing to the air raid, crashed together with total loss of crews. Their charred bodies are in the mortuary.

It is a fact that more lives are lost on training than on ops.

16.8.42
A wonderful warm day. Everything seemed transformed by the light. The corn in the field across the road looked more gold and yellow than ever; the trees seemed to shimmer in the heat, their leaves like some green fountain, and even our kites which looked so clumsy and black on the ground seemed graceful at a height.

19.8.42
We have a new pilot, Vic Page.

*

In this period Cliff was posted to another station on heavies.

Another friend John Smith, who was a keen Communist, got me to go with him to a meeting in Doncaster Town Hall at which Willie Gallagher, the Communist MP, was to speak. The hall was packed, and the message was that we should start a second front immediately to help the Russians who were fighting it out in Stalingrad. He blamed the Aston clique in the Government for being unwilling to do anything to help the Russians, and he called on us for action with the aims of "Unity and riddance of all would be Quislings." At this a roar went up from the audience which would have sent the same Quislings running from Doncaster to the South Pole if they could have heard it!

(Some time later John Smith, who was then stationed at Tempsford, lost his life while dropping supplies to the Poles in Warsaw.)

The accommodation on war-time aerodromes was not designed for comfort, as an entry in my diary shows:
"Rained all evening so decided to go out rather than stay in the hut. The damp seems to seep through the woodwork and into

your marrow and there is a constant draught."

Even so, I found it difficult to complain about my lot, which compared favourably with Army life.

*

20.8.42
Heard at dinner time today that Ernie is being sent back to Bicester with two other short fellows.

30.8.42
Went into 'C' Flight today and our crew is now complete. Vic, the pilot, is also ex-Army and he has allowed me on a few occasions already to take over the controls.

6.9.42
Gunnery over the North Sea this afternoon, up and down the stretch of coast above the Humber. It's a good feeling to be behind two powerful guns with plenty of ammunition. It's surprising all the same how few bullets find their mark. For instance, 4% is considered pretty good and 10% is exceptional. Flew again tonight in a rotten kite that nearly gave out on us.

10.9.42
Got in some high-level bombing today with fair results. I am gradually getting a grip on the new bomb sight.

I had just got into bed on arriving back when a plane roared close over our rooftop. There was a loud crash and almost instantly the sky was lit up in the direction of the mess. The blaze grew till it filled the whole horizon, while interspersed with the thuds and dull explosions of oxygen bottles going off was the quick sharp crack of bullets as the fire reached the turrets. There was one final loud explosion before the fire dwindled. Then cars began to race back and forward through the camp and people were running here and there, but somehow I had a feeling it was too late, and so it turned out next morning.

11.9.42
While on gunnery this morning I was waiting my turn to go into the rear turret when the kite gave a lurch and I fell through the fabric up to my waist. There was a strong pull on my legs from the slipstream but I managed to get back alright after a struggle.

18.9.42
Moved to Bircotes where we are to do our long day and night cross-countries. The local village is Bawtry.

1.10.42
Moved to Wing this afternoon in the ropey old kite and map-read our way down there. This is another of those highly dispersed camps. We are sleeping in a large and practically empty hut, about one-and-a-half miles from the main buildings. But who cares! We are back in the South again, thank God.

5.10.42
Our crew was put through the pressure chamber today and I was chosen to do it without oxygen. My writing went funny first, then I couldn't add or subtract and finally I passed out at 35,000 ft. Surprising thing though that right up to the moment of fainting I had the utmost confidence, an almost reckless feeling. Vic suffered from a tremendous pain in the eyes on the way down and Laurie had toothache. What wind there was inside us swelled till we thought we would burst.

6.10.42
Up early and set off on a long cross-country. The route took us from Wing to Worcester, Rhyl, Jurby, then down to South Wales doing some gunnery on the way and finally some high-

level bombing before getting back to base. The whole trip took six-and-three-quarter hours and I was grateful for a thermos and a bottle of Ovaltine tablets. Incidentally I took over the kite for a while and did alright. I reckon I could land the beggars with a bit of luck.

Moved into a new billet tonight, four of us – Vic, Laurie, Jack and self in the same room with a little stove. OK!

18.10.42

A bomb aimer on our course fell out of the entrance hatch while on a bombing run at 6,000 ft today. These hatches have a way of working themselves loose on Wimpeys, and twice already I have put my feet back into space.

While bombing also today and crouched over the sight, the bulkhead door with the full force of a 140 mph wind behind it sprung back and struck me on the beam, putting me out of action for some minutes.

23.10.42

Bombing this morning in a pretty strong wind. Terrific errors! Nearly killed some sheep. Took off again at 1 a.m. tonight. Cold as ice. Bombed first and managed to knock out some of the lights. Then as we started on our trip proper the trouble began. Intercom went u/s so back to base, and just as we got there Jason fixed it and we started off again. Although there was a wizard moon lighting the ground up with light green and blue colours, I found it very hard to recognise anything from my position and we got lost. Spent six-and-a-half hours travelling to Goole and back. Bad show!

7.11.42

On a Bulls Eye tonight at 11,000 ft. Bloody chilly. Never knew there were so many searchlights in creation. They were damn smart tonight too and picked us up without any trouble. I wonder if Jerry's as good? "Attacked" by a Mosquito that swooped only a few feet above us and was lit up by the searchlights.

20.11.42

Wizard night with a large moon. Hatch opened shortly after take-off and while I was getting down to shut it, Jason slammed the partition door in my face and I fell backwards through the gap, but luckily managed to catch the seat in my fall with one hand. I wonder how long it will be before my old enemy the hatch finally puts an end to my career?

Travelled over N. Wales to the Isle of Man where we did Infra Red bombing and it was like daylight. Took over the controls quite a bit which probably accounts for Laurie being sick. From there to Fishguard and back to Base. Pretty tired.

23.11.42

Heard today that of the original 35 on No.7 course at Penrhos only 5 are still alive.

28.11.42

Flying tonight – should be our last trip. Couldn't see a damn thing the whole five hours, but got back alright. Drank tea, smoked and ate sandwiches all the way round to keep myself from getting bored.

4.12.42

Flew for six hours tonight (definitely our last trip) and were diverted to Heyford where we had supper and a good bed without any trouble at all.
(Note: Flying Stirlings)

25.12.42

My first Xmas at home this war.

31.12.42

Arrived Waterbeach.

3.2.43
Flying is a very slow business here and so far we have only got in about eight hours. Weather not too bad but most kites are u/s.

12.2.43
Finished our training here with a loaded climb today.

Got up to 17,000 ft. A rolling sea of cloud with monstrous hills and valleys stretched away to a clear horizon. And above us the sky was deep blue, clearer than you ever see it from the ground. The wind up there was violent (about 70 mph) and there were few pinpoints right the way round because of the cloud. Passed over Ipswich with a convoy protected by barrage balloons in the estuary.

14.2.43
Arrived at Lakenheath today. 149 Squadron has the excellent motto "Fortis Nocte" (We Strike by Night) and as a badge a horseshoe with a streak of lightning running through it. Very good! This is a highly dispersed 'drome, and our Nissen hut is in amongst some pine trees. The ground is very sandy and there are trees everywhere. Excellent grub and no bull. What more could you ask? We are now in 3 Group Bomber Command.

16.2.43
Heard that Cliff is a POW. Laurie has been air-sick twice recently on cross-countries when I have had to take over, so he is no longer flying with us and we are waiting for another navigator. For the past week the weather has been wonderful; warm, clear skies, Spring in the air, almost too good to be true. Practically every day Boston, Mitchells and Venturas fly over on their daylight sweeps. Lucky swines! All we know about it is a rushing sound just over our heads and there, just for a second, are three or more kites in close formation whipping along just over the trees.

Tonight Vic is off on a second dicky trip with another crew. Hope he comes back as he's wearing my Irvine.

11.3.43

Vic went on a mining expedition to Bordeaux last night. Pretty rough do apparently. He's on again tonight.

12.3.43

Vic went to Stuttgart last night. Another of these and we should have a navigator by then and be able to settle down by ourselves. He's off again tonight.

13.3.43

Vic never returned from last night's effort, a large attack on Essen. The rest of us are stunned at the thought of never seeing him again. Hope he is a POW like Cliff.

27.3.43

We left Lakenheath five days after Vic's Essen raid, having first picked up a new navigator, Shorty, who is as disgusted with the thought of going back to conversion flights as we are. This time it is Stradishall, one of the old peacetime aerodromes with the usual camouflaged hangars etc. I am quartered with another fellow in a drying room where it is damned hot at night with pipes running all the way through it, above, below and all around us. The grub is lousy. Our new pilot is Bill Carney.

2.4.43

The usual monotony of circuits and bumps was brightened by a remarkable series of lousy landings today. Bill's weak point, apparently, is landing. Although this is our third day of circuits and bumps Bill hasn't shown that he has much grip. We came pretty near to a prang on one landing when after bashing down in an unusually hearty manner, Bill suddenly decided to take off again. We were by then halfway up the runway and in a series of sickening swerves we took off narrowly missing the roof of one of the hangers.

Went up on an air test this evening through 5,000 ft of cloud, levelling off in bright sunshine at 9,000 ft. Quite a lot of ice on the kite which sparkled and looked remarkably pretty against the deep blue sky. Cloud tops stretched away as far as the eye could see. Came down after some time and did some crafty map-reading to base. God! How I wish we were still on Blenheims.

3.4.43
More circuits today. Improving. Down to the Royal Oak in the evening where over a pipe and a glass of stout I had an interesting talk with an old Irishman who had served in the Boer War.

4.4.43
Last daylight trip today – a loaded climb. Lasted five-and-a-half hours. We reached 19,400 ft and it was the pleasantest trip I can remember. It was nice to go over the Welsh mountains again. We passed over Penrhos and I saw the house we had stayed in. Dropped some 500lb'ers on Seagull Island.

9.4.43
Went to Edinburgh this morning in an Oxford. Bumpy over the Pennines. Lunched there and came back by way of Cottesmore and Kings Lynn. Edinburgh is a remarkable looking town from the air – the castle stands out in a sea of houses. To the south is a massive line of hills, with the Firth on the other side spanned by an enormous bridge which is guarded by 20 or more barrage balloons. This was a seven-hour trip and we got back just in time for a quick tea and night flying. Got to bed at 2.30 the next morning damn tired.

10.4.43 – 16.4.43

We have done nothing but fly at night and sleep in the daytime. On the night of the 15th we went on our last trip, a Bulls Eye. Wizard night, fighters and searchlights very busy. We were caught and held by successive lots of lights right the way through London but managed three runs of infra-red bombing on Westminster Bridge. Going into the moon London was as clear as a map, a lovely sight.

Note: The crew is made up as follows:

Pilot – Bill
Navigator – Shorty
Rear Gunner – Jock
Mid-upper Gunner – Len
Wireless Operator – Jason
Flight Engineer – Paddy
Bomb Aimer – Spud

19.4.43

Arrived 218 Squadron, Downham Market, at 2 p.m., having lost our complete kit en route.

27.4.43

My birthday. Tonight we went Gardening off the island of Juiste (Frisians). Cloud pretty thick and Bill wouldn't go below the cloud to pinpoint, which is essential when dropping mines, and he seemed to panic a bit when I said that I had seen some lights. Heard a fighter being vectored on to us over the RT but Jason ballsed him up with tinsel. I saw those lights through a break in the cloud and I should think they must have been Juiste, but Bill wouldn't go down to verify our position and neither would he let me drop the mines, but came back to base like a bat out of hell.

5.5.43

Gardening again tonight. Just off Cromer on the way out we were fired at by a convoy. Urged Bill below the cloud and pinpointed easily enough on Aureland. Three searchlights coned over base to guide us back. Noticed several bats caught in the beams, some pretty high up.

7.5.43

We are in A Flight and have been allotted a brand new Mark III Stirling.

Up on fighter affiliation this morning we were chased all over the sky by a Spitfire.

Shorty and I have worked out a way to test whether Bill is windy. It's simple enough really, all Shorty has to do is to give a late ETA.

12.5.43

Set out for Duisburg tonight but had to turn back because Jason and Len couldn't get any oxygen. They had forgotten to withdraw their bobbins. Shorty and I egged Bill on to complete the trip at 10,000 or 11,000 ft but he was too damned windy to try it.

13.5.43

Off to a place called Bochum tonight, which is pretty well in the centre of the Ruhr. Carrying all incendiaries. Determined to get there at all costs. Crossed the Dutch coast off track and wandered pretty close to Antwerp. Searchlights and flak pretty strong. Beautiful moonlit night and managed to pinpoint quite easily.

The Gee went u/s sometime before reaching target area and we turned up, all unawares, over Dusseldorf. Being the only kite over the place they gave us all they'd got. Did my best to pinpoint, but was dazzled by all the lights. Bill panicked and circled about in a frantic endeavour to get out, losing height all the time. Before we left Dusseldorf we were at 6,000 ft, picked up by immense cones of 30–40 searchlights at a time and a sitting target for light, medium and heavy flak. There was plenty of it. I should think that something like 200–300 guns were firing at us at any one time. It was at this point that Bill gave the order to bale out, and I replied that if we did no one would reach the ground in one piece. Bill then said, "You bloody well fly it then" and I went up the steps and grabbed the 2nd pilot's controls. I steered a straight course and in a few minutes we had left Dusseldorf behind. Some ten minutes later Bill had recovered sufficiently to take over again.

We then passed over the southern outskirts of Essen and for several minutes we were coned by searchlights and fired at continuously. When flak hits the aircraft there is a clap like thunder and strong smell of cordite.

Finally we came to the target. The place was ablaze – immense fires covered the ground and reflected red on a great pall of smoke which hung above the town.

Meanwhile Jock (rear gunner) had obeyed the order to bale out but had pulled the ripcord too early and his parachute had partially opened, jamming him in the escape hatch. In this position, with his head, shoulders and arms out of the aircraft, he had received the full blast of the explosions for several minutes. Having bombed, I tried to get him on the intercom and had no reply so I went back to see how he was, to find him half in and half out of the hatch. He was in a dazed condition when I pulled him back in.

I then sat next to Bill. 'I' (Ink) was shaking so badly that I had to hold the throttles in position from then on.

At last we lost the searchlights and headed north into the seemingly quiet fighter belt that runs right the way from North Denmark to below Paris.

Gee still u/s but managed to pinpoint near the Zuyder Zee.

Only just enough petrol to get home. Arrived at base in the half light of early morning. TRG u/s so landed without permission. Just as I thought – everything was OK. I looked at Bill to find that he had let go the controls and had both hands over his eyes. The kite swerved suddenly to port and the next thing I knew we cut a lorry in two, killing a couple of poor blokes just back from the raid, knocked two cars for yards, partially demolished the Briefing Room, before finally pranging into the Operations Room with our right wing. A few people injured in there.

I headed for the hatch but the way was blocked by Paddy who was wielding an axe in a desperate attempt to hack his way out. I remember tapping him on the back and asking him if he had tried the hatch, and with that we all tore out of the aircraft, fully expecting it to burst into flames.

We all went to the MO who gave us two little yellow pills each which all but knocked us out before we reached the billet.

14.5.43

The kite, I'm afraid has had it. We walked around counting flak holes and there were about 100 – several extraordinarily close to where we were sitting. Len's turret has five or six holes in it, one piece of shrapnel grazing his nose on its way through. The Astro Dome was whipped away while Paddy was looking through it and Jock had a deep cut in his head. I was lucky to escape injury myself as shrapnel broke off a six inch piece of metal from my compartment which hit me on the head, but fortunately my leather helmet saved my bacon.

'I' Ink finally came to rest on the Operations Room which was below Flying Control in the Control Tower. It was here that de-briefing was taking place at the time on our crash.
Note: With hindsight, two vital things went wrong with this trip

On the way out I pinpointed our position exactly on the Dutch coast and gave a fix to Shorty, our Navigator. Through a fault in his calculations he then gave an incorrect course to our Pilot which meant that by the time we reached the Rhine we were some 20 miles north of the main stream. This in turn meant that we approached the target from completely the wrong direction. It was fortunate for us that we didn't collide with our own aircraft who, by the time we reached it, were leaving the target in a northerly direction. The second reason was that the pilot completely lost his nerve at the most crucial moment.

We were lucky to get away with it.

16.5.43

After breakfast we were told to report to the Wing Commander and when we got to his office we gave him our accounts of events to do with the raid on Bochum. I told him that we had no confidence in Bill and did not wish to fly with him again. He looked at some papers on his desk and told us that we were Bill's sixth crew and that he had crashed the lot. This was news to us, but the main thing was that he granted our request.

This interview was followed by a "Morale Flight" which went off OK. Jock is in the sick bay at the present and Bill is hanging on in the hope that we will have him back.

After our trip to Bochum the crew thought that Bill had definitely proved that he was windy about going over enemy territory, but that he was even more windy about admitting it and being classed as LMF (Lacking Moral Fibre.)

We thought that Bill would have been grounded but later, at Stradishall, we found him with another crew. I will never know for sure what happened to Bill eventually, but some months later I was in a pub chatting with a bomb aimer from another squadron who told me that he thought he had seen Bill's Stirling heading into the Channel for no apparent reason with all guns firing.

As for Jock, in the month that followed he went missing a few times and was found wandering around the fields near the aerodrome, barefoot and in his pyjamas. He was grounded and we never saw him again.

13.6.43
Posted to Stradishall again today to get a new skipper and gunner.

15.6.43
There is a pilot waiting for us here and a rear gunner. The skipper is a pilot officer by the name of Mills who seems quite a good sort. He has done three ops, thank God, so we don't have to start the second dicky business all over again. The rear gunner (John Moss) seems an excellent type. He came from 75 Squadron, Newmarket, and has ditched. We did all our circuit and bumps today.

16.6.43
Last night, about twelve o'clock, a Jerry kite (probably a Junkers 88) attacked the 'drome. All over in a few seconds. It came in very low and dropped some eggs and then peppered away with its guns. Not much damage. Saucy bugger!

25.6.43
Finished all flying and got cleared today.

26.6.43
Posted to 90 Squadron, West Wickham. New aerodrome and very dispersed. In a Nissen hut with the crew and six others. They lost six kites here last week.

27.6.43
Mining off Terschelling tonight. One mine went off on impact but otherwise OK. Our skipper Ted seems alright.

8.7.43
Went gardening off La Rochelle. Lovely moonlit night – got some good pinpoints. Fair amount of flak on the island and a little crossing the coast but nothing like the Ruhr. Ted weaved

the whole way and everyone but himself, Shorty and I were sick.

10.7.43

Once again we have a kite of our own. Lovely job, 'M' for Mother, brand new Mark III Stirling. Got the ground crew to paint our motto – "Root the Fuehrer" in large yellow letters on the side.

29.7.43

Ops Hamburg. Got within 30 miles of the target when Paddy said we hadn't enough petrol to go any further east. Had to drop the load on the coast before starting back. Damn shame as we could see the fires from the target quite clearly. Passed smack over Heligoland without any trouble. Also had a Junkers 88 on our tail but Johnny, with much abuse, got in the first burst and it disappeared.

30.7.43

Ops Remscheid – a small town in Happy Valley just east of Solingen. Passed over Dunkirk by mistake on the way out – fair amount of flak. From there it was fairly clear right up to the target as our route took us south of Cologne. The target was an impressive sight – the whole town was ablaze with a red blanket of smoke belching from it. Every so often a great white flash in the middle of it all would show where a large bomb had exploded. There were few searchlights left working and only a few guns. The sky above the town was dotted by flak puffs, which showed like balloons in the light of the fires below. Bombsight went u/s and I had to use the old finger method – laid the incendiaries smack across the centre of the blaze and then got out. We then had to pass out of the main Ruhr defences about 20 miles thick where the searchlights were busy. Saw a kite caught in a big cone and go down with sparks and flames shooting out from behind. Also saw a Jerry fighter belting along under us like a dainty silver toy.

2.8.43
Hamburg again. Engine trouble as we were about to set course, so dropped the load into the Wash, to my disgust. Abortions our speciality!

10.8.43
Nuremburg. Seven hour trip and quite tiring after the shorter efforts we have grown accustomed to. Mannheim had been attacked in force the night before and the wretched people there were kept awake by occasional kites off track and a few flares on purpose to give them the wind up. Going there and coming back the guns and searchlights of Mannheim were busy. About 9/10 cloud over the target, but managed to prang a marker. Bombing generally very scattered from what I could see, but quite a few hearty fires going. A Junkers 88 passed quite close to us with both navigation lights on but didn't see us. Quiet trip on the whole.

Engine trouble on reaching the south coast so we lobbed down at West Malling, a Mosquito station. Managed to get two hours kip in the mess before returning to base.

23.8.43
Berlin tonight, over 800 kites went, all four-engined. Not much trouble on the route there. The visibility was good so we could watch the attack as it developed. In the first six minutes the place was glowing with fires and enormous flashes were lighting up the ground.

Searchlights and flak not very intense but bags of fighters about. Making our final run up to a marker, we were suddenly attacked from very close range. It scored a few hits on the tailplane but Len and John kept their heads and brought it down. Once in flames it was picked up by searchlights and finished off by flak. Bombed dead centre and got out like bats out of hell. Counted six of our kites going down in flames.

Over the target there was a plane circling round the whole time with one of the Pathfinders (Paddy is making a running commentary, telling us where to bomb and cheering like mad whenever we scored a hit. This fellow is called the Master of Ceremonies and they use him on all the big raids.)

On the way back we got quite considerably off track crossing the Baltic and there were doubts about us ever getting back to England. Also one engine packed up for a while. We threw out my guns, ammo, etc. to lighten the load and just made Coltishall after flying for 8 hours 40 mins.

24.8.43

Left Coltishall this afternoon in another Sterling as 'M' is u/s for the time being. Tailplane and rudder full of holes. Got stoned on two pints in Cambridge.

27.8.43

Nuremberg again tonight.

30.8.43

Ops again tonight – Gladbach. Johnny went sick at last moment so we had another gunner, an Australian. We didn't fancy the idea much. Rear turret went u/s over the North Sea so we jettisoned and came back

31.8.43

Set out once more for Berlin but never got there. Engine trouble over North Sea. Jettisoned in the Wash.

1.9.43

Met John Smith in the Fountain PH Cambridge. Enjoyable evening.

8.9.43

Op tonight to petrol dump outside Boulogne carrying

6 x 1,000 lbs and 8 x 500 lb bombs. Pranged target fair and square but saw no big explosions. Fair amount of heavy and light flak but no fighters.

15.9.43

Bombed a rubber factory near Montlucon (Central France). Had to run in pretty low because of cloud. Target well ablaze by the time we got there and dense clouds of smoke (we could smell the rubber) rising high above it. The aircraft was shaken considerably by large explosions on our run in, which I thought at the time was flak but turned out to be blast from our bombs. We were heading into an enormous pillar of black smoke when Shorty, who was in the second dicky's seat, noticed two other kites converging on us. He pushed the stick forward and, with the steepness of the dive, fell forward on to it and lost control. All four engines cut at the same time and we went screaming down this pillar of smoke till at about 3,000 ft Ted pulled us out. Otherwise the trip was uneventful, flying for six hours in bright moonlight. Coming home I looked back and saw the smoke, dark and enormous in the moonlight, reaching up to about 10,000 ft, like a great mushroom.

16.9.43

Ops again tonight, this time to a place called Modane, which is one of the four vital railway links between Germany, France and Italy. The target was in a valley with mountains rising steeply on either side to about 10,000 ft. About 10 miles East is the Italian border and about 60 miles North the same border joins Switzerland.

Lovely night with a wizard moon which lit up the ground like daylight. On the way out we passed 30 miles to port of Montlucon, which we could see quite clearly still glowing from last night's effort. After passing Lyons we came to the high country, a sight I shall not easily forget. Great jagged peaks and ridges stood out hard and clear, with valleys mostly thrown into shadow. We seemed to be flying very close to the tops and I thought what an uncomfortable place it would be to land on.

The first bombs were falling as we began our run-in to the target, flying up a valley. I wondered what the echoes must have sounded like as we were all carrying high explosives. Saw Mont Blanc quite clearly 50 miles on our starboard beam as we came out.

Noticed a strange thing crossing the coast on the way home. A round of incendiary flak shot up vertically into the sky till it reached our level, when it began to move parallel to the ground. Shortly afterwards there was a great flash and an aircraft, presumably one of ours, fell down in flames. Back at de-briefing the Intelligence Officer said it was a new radio-directed shell which can be vectored on to aircraft.

Eight hour trip.

22.9.43

Ops Hanover. Got to about 8,000 ft over base while waiting to set course when another of our kites (K) which was at the same height and not far from us, suddenly caught fire. She kept a steady course for about a minute, then seemed to hover before shooting down like a stone. Before she reached the ground the fire had spread along both wings, the engines had disintegrated and were blazing away in separate fires. Then the kite crashed with all its incendiaries and bombs. Surprisingly, the mid-upper gunner survived.

We never got to Hanover as we had engine trouble not far from the Dutch coast.

23.9.43

To Mannheim in 'L' Love. Target pretty hot, lit up for miles around by fighter flares and fires. Noticed for the first time lines of yellow flares dropped by Jerry to show our route in and out of the target. And there were the usual two walls of searchlights, with us and the fighters in between. Came off pretty lightly with one hole in Len's turret and a few dents in the old bus.

Damn strain on the eyes these long trips. Lost one kite over the target and another with Perce in it was badly hit. Perce and the W/Op baled out over the target, rear gunner dead in turret and the others came back on two engines and pranged just inside the East coast.

27.9.43

Hanover again. Just as we were about to taxi on to the runway for take-off, 'M' went u/s (engines again). So we dashed into 'Q' and set course as we took off. A good many fighter flares on the way and saw a fair number of ours shot down, but no trouble ourselves until the bombing run, when just as I was about to press the tit I heard John's voice say "Fighter" and heard the rattle of guns and saw a stream of tracer shooting under the bomb window. Dropped the load (19 cans) onto an inferno of fire below and weaved away out of the target. We damaged the fighter, an ME 110, which cleared off into the darkness.

Hanover is one of the toughest targets I have yet been to, with enormous sheet of flame and smoke, the sky filled with flak puffs, searchlights and markers. Best prang I have seen yet. Near Emden saw one of our kites shot down by a Jerry fighter who followed it down, firing all the way. One kite pranged near Haverhill – mid-upper gunner and engineer OK. Another came back with rear gunner badly wounded and landed at Stradishall.

Apart from the normal dangers there is the added one in these days of big raids of hitting one of our own kites in the dark. On average once, sometimes two or three times on a trip, we have all but pranged another bomber.

For this reason I spend a good deal of time sitting next to Ted, which, as it turned out, is just as well. Coming back to base from Hanover the weather closed in until nothing could be seen but an occasional light below in the blackness. I happened to glance out of Ted's window and saw an enormous black shape sweeping towards us. Ted hadn't seen it and I hadn't time to warn him, so I heaved the stick back as hard as I could and we just made it.

28.9.43

Took a look at 'Q' this morning and find that one of the tailplanes is riddled, and the starboard wing and petrol tank have a few holes as well.

13.10.43

Moved camp today to Tuddenham, which is near to Mildenhall. Flew here. As usual in moving I lost some kit, a pair of flying boots. Hell! This place is sandy and fairly thickly wooded like Lakenheath. Out with John and Shorty tonight and spent a pleasant evening in the Bull at Barton Mills.

17.10.43 – 30.10.43

No ops since our last leave. Deadly weather – fogs and frosts.

Although the Squadron had flown two Gardening trips this month, we have managed to lose three kites. Our crew who were in our hut at West Wickham ditched on their first trip, shot down by one of our own ships. Picked up after six hours. W/Op missing. Good start.

The other crew were shooting up their old OTU at Benson when they hit something and were all killed. Another crew were landing in daylight with three engines, but judged wrongly and pranged about a quarter of a mile short of the runway. There was an enormous explosion – the usual fire with ammo and explosion bottles exploding all over the place. Mid-upper still living.

10.11.43

Today Rogers and crew and three others had a wing clipped on a fighter. They are 20 ft down in marshy land.

11.11.43
Tomlin (who ditched on his first trip) was on a Bulls Eye last night when their kite crashed near Stradishall. He and the mid-upper both killed; the others baled out and are OK.

13.11.43
McInnes finished his tour today. Saw him off at the Bull.

18.11.43
Mannheim tonight. A lot of flak but didn't see one fighter. Cold as hell – minus 30 degrees at 15,000 ft. Tea from my thermos froze in cup before I could drink it.

*

A favourite haunt in our spare time was the Bull at Barton Mills, which was a comfortable Georgian coaching inn near the A11. There was a cheerful feel about the place and it became the haunt of RAF personnel as it was situated close to three aerodromes. There was a good fire going when it was cold and the air was full of cigarette smoke, loud talk and laughter. To get off your bike on a black night and enter this building was a heartening experience.

In December '43 we had an interesting talk from a gunner who had escaped from Stalag VIIIB. which was near Breslau in East Germany. He knew my friend Cliff, who was a prisoner in this camp, and said that he had escaped but had been re-captured. This gunner spent several months escaping, and picked up a lot of useful information about German industry on the way. He travelled by way of Rostock to Sweden and talked three Danish seamen into leaving the ship with him when close to the Swedish shore.

*

Penrhos April 1942

Medals

Top row: Ken (Gunner), Bill Passlow (Skipper) Jimmy Young (Nav)
Self (Bomb Airmen) Eric (Flight Engineer)
Bottom row: Burch (Rear Gunner) Poggy (Wlop)

23.8.1943 Stirlings of 90 Sqdr, West Wickham. Lining up for take off to Berlin.

Spud after a hard day 1943/44

SPUD 1944 When he was flying on raids.

19.11.43

Set off for Leverkeusen but 'M' did it again – oil leak this time. Jettisoned in Wash.

22.11.43

Berlin tonight. Plenty of high cloud and several electrical storms. Our compasses did some queer things about 20 minutes before we were due at the target, but at zero hour we could see some markers dropping and the clouds lit up some miles away. We went there and bombed through a gap in the cloud. I saw a part of the city lit up by incendiaries and the continuous flashing of bombs. Before we left the clouds had been turned to a dull red by the fires below. There was quite a lot of flak but not accurate. On the way back, while Shorty was taking a shot in the astro dome, we were picked up by some very accurate flak batteries who chased us out of their area.

1.12.43

Set out for the Skagerak (Baltic). Flew low over the North Sea while it was still light and could see the three other kites from the Squadron on each side and in front of us. Then as it became dark we climbed to get above some cloud and the compasses went haywire. But this time we were over Denmark and Jason dropped some pamphlets. Ted decided it would be foolish to go the whole distance with the compasses as they were, and so back to base.

9.12.43

About lunchtime the fog lifted to about 400 ft and we took off. A short but hair-raising trip, circling with six other kites over Tempsford before making a split-arse landing. Briefed straight away to go to a place called Blida (Algeria) carrying cans of dynamite and three agents. Then at the last moment they decided to cancel one of the six crews – and blow me, we lost. (Note: At this point John, our rear gunner, finished his tour and was replaced by Fred.)

19.2.44

Ops tonight. Gardening in Kiel harbour. The min. force of Lancasters and Halifaxes are going to Leipzig. Dirty night when we started, drizzle and low cloud, but we got off alright and soon whipped up into a clear sky. Journey fairly uneventful. Not much cloud over Denmark and fair amount of flak but the fighters were too busy with the main force to bother about us. Damn cold.

3.3.44

We are now doing the same kind of work as Tempsford during moon periods. Tonight with a horned moon and clear skies we set out to drop supplies in the Haute Savoie. Crossed the French cost without incident and then dropped down to 2,000 ft for the long journey inland. Gee faded out pretty soon, but the Met winds were pretty good and map-reading was like daylight. Found the place and the reception committee who flashed the letter we had been given (N), and dropped our containers. On the way back we got off track a bit and were shot at by a couple of light flak guns, but otherwise no trouble. Bed about 6 this morning.
(Note: We were dropping arms and equipment to the French Resistance.)

4.3.44

Another drop tonight – nearer Switzerland this time. Got a trifle off track on the way in. Stooged straight over a defended aerodrome near Bourges. I was sitting by Ted when suddenly three searchlights flashed on to us from in front, and a second later three or four guns opened up with coloured tracers. If they had held their fire for a few seconds longer I think they would have got us, but as it was we were just bumped about a bit. Shells coming over us exploded on a hillside just in front. Len and Fred returned fire and put out one of the lights. Got to the area alright but cloud prevented us from finding the committee, so we had to bring the load back.

11.3.44

Down to the Bordeaux area but couldn't see the deck for cloud.

13.3.44

Gardening off La Rochelle tonight in bright moonlight. Gee went u/s halfway across the Channel and we strayed a bit towards the end. Flew over Caen which is supposed to be heavily defended – could see every house and street like daylight, but not a shot fired.

15.3.44

Bombed the marshalling yards at Amiens. Fair amount of opposition. 'P' missing.

17.3.44

Afternoon off. Just before going out, Shorty and I discovered that we have finished our tour.

In the evening we went to the Bull in Barton Mills with Doris, Pam, Phyl and the crew and celebrated in a big way, helped by some Irishmen and the Padre, it being St. Patrick's Day.

*

A Note about the Maquis:
It was decided to take Stirlings off the raids on German cities because the Lancasters taking part in these raids in increasing numbers had a higher ceiling and there was a distinct risk of their bombs hitting our aircraft.

The French Resistance (the Maquis) were being supplied with agents, dropped, and picked up by crews from Tempsford. Our job was to drop supplies – mainly arms and ammunition, to the Maquis. The BBC would broadcast coded messages at certain times of the day which indicated the time and place of the drop. I heard a few of these messages on the wireless and they were generally on the following lines: "Aunt Jane would like to come for tea at 4 p.m." etc.

Trips were made at low level and required a high degree of accurate navigation as the Reception Committee had no wish to advertise their presence to the Germans, and could only signal with torches or bonfires.

*

Note: It worked out alright with our pilot Ted, but he had his peculiarities. One was that he never failed to corkscrew his way across enemy territory. Another was that he was rather deaf, so that all orders given to him by the gunners or myself, on which our lives depended (i.e. fighter or searchlight control) had to be shouted.

And finally his sight was rather suspect. For instance, flying over France on a clear night he took violent evasive action to avoid what he thought was a searchlight but turned out to be the Milky Way! On another occasion, after a long and tiring flight we were circling base and Ted had switched on his TRG to get landing permission when, once more, he took violent evasive action to avoid an intruder with its lights on (which was their custom) – but this time it turned out to be a star. Unfortunately, our conversation from then on was relayed to the control tower, and on landing we were met by a very irate Group Captain.

But Ted's strong point was that precisely because of these handicaps he was not over-cautious, and after our experiences with Bill this came as a great relief.

And finally, he was a smashing bloke and an excellent pilot.

*

I thought it appropriate at this stage to add some explanatory notes.

We lived in an age of inventions and here are some that we used on the bombers I flew in:

1. Aircraft flying low at night were liable to run into balloon or electric cables, so we were fitted with a rail on the leading edge of both wings, with a powerful cutter that was activated by a detonator.

2. My original bomb sight was a rigid instrument which took no account of the angle of the aircraft at the moment of release. The new sight was fitted with a small rectangular plate of glass which was gyroscopically controlled. A faint red cross was lit up on the glass and the object was to get the target running along the longer arm of the cross and releasing the load when the target reached the point where the two arms crossed.

3. Packets of 'window' were loaded into my compartment before take-off, and these were pushed out of a chute at odd intervals over enemy territory. These filled the sky as they fluttered to the ground and baffled enemy radar. Each strip of window was about the shape of those coloured paper strips with which we used to make paper chains at Christmas, only they were silver-coloured and had a metallic look.

4. Fishpond. This was a device fitted into the wireless operator's compartment with a small glass screen. Aircraft appeared as green dots.

5. The W/Op also operated another device whose name I forget. By tuning in to German ground control who were directing the movements of their fighters, it was possible to broadcast a gigantic raspberry on the same wavelength,

making it impossible for them to communicate with each other. The raspberry came from the noise of our engines. It was marvellous to hear their voices screaming with rage when this gadget was turned on!

6. If a petrol tank caught fire, an aircraft was normally doomed. So a self-sealing tank was invented which prevented loss of fuel and the chances of fire were much reduced.

7. H.2.S A navigational aid designed to give a picture of the ground on a screen –it could not be jammed.

8. Gee. Another navigational aid designed to give your position which could be jammed.

9. Oboe. This came in towards the end of the war. If I remember correctly the aircraft travelled down a beam making an intermittent sound. When the sound became continuous it meant that you had reached a certain spot in the sky – i.e. over the target.

10. Fido. This was a device to dispense fog and was installed at the end of the runway on which you were landing. An example of this was the one at Woodbridge. We landed there twice.

11. Pilots and navigators were issued with Swiss watches which were proof against temperature changes and were accurate to the second. They were set at briefing.

12. I was issued with Polaroid dark glasses which improved my vision considerably when flying in daylight.

13. Escape kits and photos. We all carried escape photos, very similar to passport photos, and taken of us wearing a civil-

ian jacket. The kits were issued before take-off and contained, as far as I can remember, a minute compass, foreign money, a silk handkerchief with a map of Europe printed on it, and water-purifying tablets.

I have no doubt there were a dozen other inventions I have forgotten about, but the list gives an idea of the inventiveness of the RAF.

Briefing

This took place in a large Nissen but several hours before take-off on a raid. At one end of the hut was a low stage with a large map of Europe over which curtains were drawn. The crew had no idea where they were going and sat awaiting events with a distinct air of anticipation.

The Station Commander unveiled the map on which tapes showed the route to and from the target. He explained the purpose of the raid, occasionally read out a message from our Chief, "Bomber" Harris, and wished us good luck. The various specialist senior officers then gave vital details – i.e. colours of the day, times, exact route, TI (target indicator) colours, bomb load, wireless frequencies, the position of convoys, the weather, etc.

Notes were taken, maps marked with routes, we had a supper of bacon and eggs and got all our gear ready.

De-Briefing

This occurred on our return to base when each individual crew was interviewed by an Intelligence Officer. We were red-eyed from staring into the dark, tired, with the marks of the oxygen masks still on our faces and the taste of oxygen still in our mouths and our hair flattened by our helmets when we were interviewed. While this went on we drank coffee laced with rum, and smoked fags.

The Pathfinders

I always had the greatest admiration for the Pathfinders and it was noticeable that with their arrival we began to bomb accurately and cause real damage to the enemy. I volunteered to join them but was not accepted, presumably because I was not up to their high standard.

They operated by identifying the target at low level, flying in Mosquitos which dropped a target indicator (TI) on to the objective. Meanwhile their high-level Lancasters circled above and kept dropping further TIs on to the target until the raid was over. The Germans were no fools and soon caught on to the idea of dropping similar flares well away from the target. The Pathfinders then introduced the Master of Ceremonies whose job was to cheer you on and tell you which were the true or false TIs. All this made the job of the bomb aimer much easier as we were told at briefing simply to bomb a particular colour (red, green, etc.) which were so bright that they could be seen from miles away. In the meantime the Pathfinders became a prime target for fighters, and I think there is no doubt at all that they carried out the most dangerous tasks performed by Bomber Command. The crews I served with regard the target area as the most dangerous and spent as little time there as possible.

A remarkable example of their skill became apparent one night when the target was completely obscured by 10/10 cloud. We were told to drop our bombs on the spot where the TIs entered the cloud, which meant that the Pathfinders had to allow for our speed, height and direction, as well as the trajectory of our bombs in their calculations and as photos proved, the next day they were spot on.

Maps

As a map-reader and bomb aimer, I found two maps particularly useful. The first was a map to cover your route, and the second was a target map. Both were excellent.

Navigation

It soon dawned on me when I was being trained as an Observer that once you were airborne in those days you were absolutely on your own. You couldn't drop anchor, ask anyone the way or, when on ops, break radio silence except to give a Mayday call. At night a blackout operated all over Europe, which made identification of objects on the ground very difficult. On moonlit nights you discovered that you could see best looking into the moon, and on cloudless nights without a moon you could, with practice, distinguish coastlines, large rivers and lakes, and you knew from the amount of flak going up that you were getting close to ships, towns or aerodromes, and that gave you a clue.

Navigation depended on a knowledge of wind speed and direction – both altered as you climbed and would also change on your way to and from the target. Also it was important that you arrived at the target at the correct height and time. In daylight it was easier to work out your position, provided the ground wasn't obscure by cloud or mist.

There were two aids, Gee and H2S which were designed to help the navigator. Both gave pictures on a small screen, but Gee was usually jammed by the Germans and was of no use over their territory, and H2S produced a vague picture which was not easy to identify.

In practice navigation for us worked out like this:

You set course from base using the information given by the Met Officer with the first turning point at, say, Cromer. With the Norfolk coast directly below me, I would identify our exact position and relay this information to the navigator. Suppose for instance we were over Sheringham or Mundesley, the navigator would be able to calculate the correct wind speed and direction and work out our course for the Dutch coast. And this process would be repeated throughout the journey. So map-reading was a major and constant part of my job, and fortunately I had been well trained in this skill as an Observer. I suspect that people who couldn't map-read could quite easily run out of fuel and end up in the North Sea.

Photography in the RAF

The official camera was in a fixed position under the aircraft and, on bombers, it was designed to take photographs of the ground during the bombing run. It took a number of pictures with the point of impact in the centre of the middle frame all taken, in theory, with the aircraft flying straight and level. In practice it didn't always work out like that as evasive action was often being taken at the crucial moment. These cameras operated automatically on opening the bomb doors; a flare, released with the bombs, lit up the ground with a giant flash when flying at night.

The photos themselves include a lot of information such as date, height, direction, target, bomb load, name of pilot, aircraft letter and squadron.

Private photography was pretty tricky to carry out for several reasons. It was only possible in daylight and then all pictures had to be taken while on the move and through thick perspex. Films were difficult to get and mine were supplied by the Photography Section who, for a small consideration, would make up and process films for those in the know.

The camera I used had originally belonged to my elder brother Andrew, who was in the army and was killed in Belgium at the time of Dunkirk. It was a Kodak pocket camera with leather bellows and a viewfinder that required one to look vertically downwards to get a forward view. This made it tricky to operate in the confined space of a bombing compartment, but I managed to take a few aerial shots, some of which came out quite well.

Flying Conditions in Wartime Bombers

As far as I was concerned as a bomb aimer/front gunner I was always positioned in a small compartment in the nose of the aircraft. Over my head were two turret doors and a metal bar. To get into the turret I opened the doors, grabbed the bar with both hands and lifted myself into the turret. I would then shut the doors to behind me in the very cramped space available, and I was then able to fire my guns. As most actions involving the use of guns took place in a matter of seconds, I generally found that by the time I was ready to fire it was all over. I did however manage to get a burst in when flying at low level over an aerodrome in France one night, and helped to put out a searchlight.

Down below the turret in my compartment there was a bomb sight, parachute, maps, thermos flask and rations and piles of window, so that there was very little room to move about. In addition, I was plugged in to the intercom and to the oxygen. Temperatures could get very low, owing to air getting in via the turret, and I can remember once pouring tea from a thermos which then turned to ice in the cup. My flying equipment included a leather helmet with earphones, which was strapped under the chin. Attached to one side of the helmet was an oxygen mask which also incorporated a speaker which could be switched on and off as required. A parachute, Mae West and escape kit were issued before each flight. Other equipment included three pairs of gloves – silk, soft wool and leather – fur-lined flying boots and Irvine jacket and a large woollen polo-neck jumper. As they aged, these jumpers often stretched to the knees, and I have seen many an aircrew do an impromptu dance wearing one of these in the locker room before take-off. Sometimes two men would get into one jumper and do a tango!

There was also a whistle in case you ditched in the dark, an inner and outer suit (something like a boiler suit in shape) and finally a similar shaped suit which could be plugged in like an electric blanket. I never used this last one as it considerably hampered my movements.

On take-off in Stirlings I sat next to the pilot until the wheels were up, and then went down to my compartment where I either lay down or crouched, depending on what I was doing. On landing I sat next to the pilot and pulled the four throttles back when he gave the order to "cut". In my compartment, when the pilot cork-screwed (as happened a good deal on our first tour) I was pressed to the floor or sides and became almost weightless in a dive. Fortunately I was not prone to air sickness but it did make map-reading rather difficult.

Our aircraft were not pressurised and you had to pinch your nose and blow to relieve the pressure on your eardrums. But to compensate for all this I had the best forward and downward view of anyone in the aircraft. With the bulkhead door open I could look back and see the pilot and flight engineer immediately behind and above me. They were moderately warm and needed fewer flying clothes than I did. Behind them came the navigator and wireless operator in the warmest positions of all, then the mid-upper gunner in about the same sort of temperature as myself. Finally came the rear gunner, hidden by the metal back of his turret, in the coldest and loneliest position of all. Both he and the mid-upper gunner had to keep alert the whole time, staring out into the dark and identifying dark aircraft against a dark sky. As far as possible they had to be careful not to lose their night vision by staring at lights, and they had to constantly sweep the sky with their turrets and guns. The front and mid-upper turrets were mounted with two Browning machine guns each, while the rear gunner had four. The Brownings fired 303 bullets (these were the same bullets which we used in our Army rifles in 1939) interspersed with tracer and armour piercing ammunition, while German fighters were armed with cannons which had a greater range and were more devastating.

The German night fighters almost always had the advantage over our bombers. They had the edge over us in height, speed and fire power, and could pick us out silhouetted against the bright lights below. This is why we were so vulnerable over the target area, and it was only due to the skill of our two gunners that we managed to fight off the attacks that were made on us.

As well as all this, the aircraft were equipped with a large inflatable dinghy capable of holding all seven of us. This in its turn was fitted with a sea anchor, a kite which provided an aerial when flown, and a waterproof transmitter. When a handle was turned on the transmitter it gave out the Mayday signal.

And talking of Mayday signals, we were once approaching base at night after an Op when this signal came over the air with a request for help from a bomb aimer whose pilot had been killed but who had managed to fly the aircraft back over his base. He wanted to know whether he should try and land or put the aircraft on automatic pilot and bale out. He was advised to land and was successfully brought down by ground control, a remarkable feat by all concerned and particularly to have managed it in the dark. We had kept radio silence throughout this drama and were now free to get on with our own landing procedures.

We were also fitted with a Verey pistol and were given cartridges with the colours of the day before take-off. In our case we never found this was of any help if we passed over a convoy escorted by the Royal Navy, as they invariably took a pot shot at us and occasionally brought one down.

As more equipment was invented (Gee, Fishpond, H2S etc.) space became more confined and really, looking back on the whole business, I realise that we were a pretty agile bunch of young men. And finally, the rations with which we were issued before Ops included items which were in very short supply for civilians, such as a bar of Cadbury's milk chocolate, barley sugar and glucose tablets.

"Wakey Wakey" pills were also issued but I found them quite useless and if I couldn't give them away I used to flush them down the lavatory.

*

I have added some excerpts from my diaries to explain what I did on leave; whether I hitch-hiked, went to the cinema, etc.

There was severe petrol rationing during the war and private cars were few and far between, so that transport was limited and trains were used to an extent which is hard to imagine today.

There follows a description of a week's leave in February 1941. At that time my mother lived with my younger brother, John, in East Bedfont, Middx. My Aunt Kay (my father's sister), who was a health visitor, lived with her widowed mother in Maidenhead, Berks. Uncle Hedley was my father's youngest brother, and he lived in Slough, Bucks. He had formerly managed a silk factory in Canton, China (until driven out by the Japanese), but when the war started he was directed to work in an engineering factory in Slough, operating machinery. He was married to Edith, a Canadian, who he first met in China, and who I always considered to be one of the nicest people I knew. She worked as a teacher in Slough. Donald and Rhena were their two children.

In 1934, when my family came to England from China, my elder brother Andrew and I were left in the care of my Aunt Kay. My mother, father and brother John returned to China, where my father died in 1937. My mother and John then came back to England and settled in East Bedfont.

In the meantime I had left school and obtained work in Maidenhead as a junior clerk with an estate agent, earning ten shillings (50p) a week, and so as to be near my work I continued to live with my Aunt Kay.

My leaves then were divided between my two homes, Maidenhead and East Bedfont, but as I had a keen eye for landscape I must confess that of the two I preferred Maidenhead.

A week's leave taken while I was stationed at Penrhos, North Wales.

*

9.2.41

Cold and wet sort of day. It takes trains longer to get from Bangor to Crew than from Crewe to London.

10.2.41

(East Bedfont) Cooked my own breakfast and lounged about most of the day.

11.2.41

Went to London with Mum and had dinner at a Lyons Corner House, a very swell place and highly decorated. Two actresses sat with us at a table and talked languidly about the qualities of various makes of lipstick. Went to a flick after dinner and after that Mum went home.

Left to myself I followed one of my favourite occupations, which is rummaging about in second-hand shops, where I bought a good watercolour which has no signature but looks much like the style of Augustus John. Also got a very pretty little Japanese woodcut.

I then for the first time went to a ballet, *The Gates of Kiev*. I found the music very disappointing.

13.2.41

John passed his RAF medical and is to start his training as an Observer sometime this summer. Celebrated by going to the flicks where we saw Hatters Castle.

14.2.41

Cycled to Maidenhead this morning on Mum's old bike – a fine day. I swear there is nothing like Maidenhead country. Had a terrific dinner, after which I went for a walk with Kay round by Pinkney's Green and along the track by the Copse. Some Italian POWs were clearing a great space in the Thicket near Pinkney's Green.

Coming down from the Copse there were some Eton lads

beagling. The were accompanied by an excited pack of hounds. Their quarry was a hare, a minute dot in the distance travelling at a rate of knots.

John arrived during the afternoon and this evening we went out and had some draught cider in a pub.

15.2.41

Breakfast in bed brought up by good old Kay. While in bed I found great satisfaction in smoking a Woodbine and glancing at the paintings I have hung on the walls.

Went for a walk with John, to discover that Maidenhead has not changed a scrap.

Went to the Hedley's this afternoon. Donald is much the same and looks very wise with his glasses – and indeed he is what he looks and knows a damn sight more than I do about most things, and has even composed a bit of music. I expect he will shortly be snatched away to heaven.

Rhena has grown a lot and seldom cries – a nice kid. She pulled out one of her teeth at teatime and put it down on her plate without saying a word.

Uncle Hedley still works hard at the factory in Slough, making parts for Stirling Bombers. Apparently he is doing some very responsible work there but has had no rise in pay. I must say I admire his adaptability. Got back to Maidenhead about 7 p.m.

16.2.41

Spent most of the day eating and tidying up. Sadly, my leaves ends today, and Kay saw me off at the station.

In London a couple of tarts, pissed as coots and singing bawdy songs, were in the same carriage in the Underground. Managed to get a seat on a very crowded train. Our compartment was occupied by a drunk Canadian sergeant, two civilians and myself. The sergeant occupied three quarters of the compartment.

*

Another entry regarding leave at a later date follows:-

1.4.42
Was told by my Aunt Kay that her mother (my grandmother) was seriously ill, and it so happened that I had been given some leave before being posted to Wratting Common, so I set out with all my gear (extra gear including my flying equipment) for Maidenhead. My grandmother died on the 3rd April, and I spent the next few days helping Kay to sort things out.

3.4.42
(On leave in Maidenhead.) This morning I spent in Grandma's room, sticking old photographs into albums. Then Kay arrived and I went out for a walk. In the evening at about six it was raining steadily. Shortly after, and very peacefully, Grandma's spirit left the house, through the rain and cloud and into the clear sunlight above.

11.4. 42
Went to the flicks in Caernarvon, although no sooner entered than we wished ourselves outside again. A thick brown cloud of tobacco smoke hung heavily over the audience, and the heat was almost unbearable. Entering the fresh air again was like diving into the sea on a sultry day.
(Note: I went to the cinema (or flicks) as often as I could during the war, and all through that time smoking was prevalent and was taken for granted.)

12.4.44
Got to Liverpool St. Station where I asked a Military Policeman if he knew which train I should catch and he said, "Yes mate, that's it just pulling out." With that I ran across and a

young woman in Land Army uniform leaned out of a carriage window and said that she had better give me a hand or I would miss the train. And that is how I met Marguerite Buhl. Her mother, who came from Southern Ireland, had died in 1940, and her father, Henri, who was born in Alsace, was a chef. He lived in Clapham and provided a home for his two daughters, Marie and Marguerite. During the previous week his flat had been bombed and Marguerite, who had been to Marie's wedding, had also spent some time moving various articles from the old flat to the new one in Deauville Mansions. When I met her she was returning to her Land Army hostel in Halstead.

Just to finish off a most interesting day I found that I was on the wrong train, but I managed to get to Wratting Common later in the day.

It didn't take me long to fall in love with Marguerite, and I met her as often as possible in the ensuing weeks.

12.4.44

The first ten days at Wratting Common were spent listening to other people's lectures, and then I started to give my own. The basic idea is to give aircrew who haven't yet been on Ops the benefit of your experience. One thing which I find rather odd is that the RAF do not appear to give any special consideration to searchlight control. The method which we worked out for ourselves was very simple and usually worked. On the principle that a searchlight can traverse the sky much faster than any aircraft can move, our method worked out like this:

The bomb aimer sees a searchlight coming directly towards the aircraft and it is so close that there is not time for manoeuvre. At the crucial moment he gives the order to the pilot to turn into the light, and once through to alter course immediately. There are several other little tricks of the trade which I passed on in my lectures. But I must confess that I am a poor lecturer and found the whole thing pretty boring.

18.6.44

To Clapham in the afternoon. People excited about a new German device called a "Doodlebug", which is a large (2000 lb) flying bomb, jet propelled, that has been pestering London for the last three days. They fly over at about 2,000–3,000 ft at a speed of roughly 400 mph and make a loud noise. When it reaches its target the engine cuts, noise stops and down she comes.

In the Underground I met a small boy with blood on his face and two women who were crying as they had just been bombed out by one of these confounded things.

All this made me pretty anxious about Marguerite. She was alright though, and at tea I saw one of these bombs tear across the window followed by two fighters.

Went out for a pint with Marguerite, Pop and Frank* in the evening, and a few bombs came along to keep us company. Saw one suddenly stop not far away and dive to earth, which resulted in a cloud of brown smoke.

During the night I saw one travel across the sky looking something like a kite on fire. They followed it with searchlights but didn't shoot.

10.11.44

Posted to Woolford Lodge.

18.11.44

Married Marguerite Buhl at St. Mary's RC Church, Clapham.

18.11.44 – 25.11.44

The week we spent at the George went with remarkable speed. Drank a fair amount and ate colossal meals of the best grub I have ever tasted.

---

* I was engaged to Marguerite Buhl, Pop was her father and Frank her brother-in-law.

Our window looked out onto Battle Abbey and the rolling woodland country that leads to Beachy Head. I have never enjoyed myself so much in the whole of my life.

The George Hotel was a comfortable Georgian coaching inn, rather like the Bull at Barton Mills, which is mentioned earlier. It was run by a family who had the gift of making their guests feel most welcome. The bill, which we kept, was made up as follows:-

1 week's board and residence @ 3½ guineas	£7 7s 0d
2 afternoon teas @ 1.3d	1s 3d
(should be £2s 6d)	
8 pints of Brown Ale @ 1.6d	12s 0d
6 Sherries @ 2/-	12s 0d
1 Cider	9d
2 pints M B @ 1/-	2s 0d
Electric fire	7s 6d
	£9 2s 6d
Breakfasts in bed	7s 6d
	£9 10s 0d

30.12.44
Posted to Conversion Unit, Bottesford. Flying in Lancasters for the first time.

17.1.45
Finished our training at Bottesford and were given a week's leave. A few hours after returning to the aerodrome I had a telegram saying that the flat in Clapham had been badly damaged by a V2, so I went straight back to London to find Marguerite in bed at a friend's house, having been injured by flying glass but still alive, thank God.
Note: The V2 had landed in the "well" at the rear of the building and directly below where Marguerite was at the time of the explosion, while her sister, Marie, was in a bedroom with her baby. Although their flat was on the second floor, the force of the explosion was such that large splinters of glass were

driven clean through the plaster and right into the brickwork. The ceilings, which were thick moulded plaster, fell to the floor, and it took my brother-in-law and I several days to clear the decks by the simple process of throwing the debris out of the windows. Had Marguerite been struck by any of the larger splinters she would have been severely injured, if not killed outright. But, by some miracle, she got away with several cuts to her face and shoulders made by smaller splinters, while Marie and the baby were frightened but unhurt.

7.2.45
Posted to 149 Squadron, now at Methwold. The crew:
- Bill Passlow – Australian Pilot
- Butch – Rear Gunner from Devon
- Pappy – New Zealand W/Op
- Eric – Flight Engineer (a Londoner)
- Ken – Mid-Upper Gunner (Northampton)
- Self – Bomber Aimer

22.2.45
Did our first Op – a daylight trip to Osterfeld to bomb a benzine factory. Flak pretty accurate with holes in the nose, wings and fuselage. Also, as I opened the bomb doors flak cut the main bombing cable, so the bombs wouldn't drop. Coming back we tried all kinds of positions to get rid of the bombs, and finally found that by diving the wires touched, and so jettisoned in the North Sea. A lovely clear day.

23.2.45
To Gelsenkirchen (Happy Valley) and bombed in cloud at 21,000 ft. Diverted to Acclington.

25.2.45
Went to Kamen, just west of the Ruhr to bomb an oil refinery. Did a grand tour of the Happy Valley on this op. Lovely day.

Fair amount of flak but nothing like we used to get. Terrific fighter escort.

26.2.45
Up early this morning and bombed an oil refinery at Dortmund. No trouble and another lovely day. Saw Cologne Cathedral as clear on the way back. The Happy Valley is uncannily peaceful these days.

28.2.45
Ops Gelsenkirchen.

1.3.45
Kamen again. Very different technique on these daylight trips. We fly in loose formations, either in V's or in boxes, each formation with a GH Leader. The three behind bomb on the leader. I find loose formation a good idea, as weaving is possible and bombing remarkably accurate.

4.3.45
Woken up in the early hours this morning and were briefed to bomb the railway yards at Wanne Eickel. Since our armies have reached the Rhine, Jerry troops are being rushed to trouble spots wherever possible by rail. We are trying out a new formation today, more compact than the usual string of V's and boxes. We were No.3 in the last Vick. A thick layer of cloud covered the target, with brilliant sunshine above. A certain amount of inaccurate flak. Crossing the English coast on the way home we ran into thick cloud and drove through it in blinding rain, till we reached base.

6.3.45
Ops Salzbergen.

7.3.45

In the afternoon we were briefed for a night raid on Dessau, about 40 miles SW of Berlin. Set out over France in broad daylight and it became dark just as we entered the Ruhr. Cologne was ablaze and the gunflashes were reflecting on the cloud. We passed by a number of raids going on in the Happy Valley and it was quite like old times to see the target indicators, flak, flares and all the hundred and one other mysterious lights that come out on a night trip. Our Gee and H2S were both u/s so we went round on dead reckoning and kept remarkably close to track all the way. The target was well ablaze when we left it – a good prang. Saw a number of kites (about 15) shot down and saw one fighter ourselves. Felt really worn out when we got back. This was a nine-and-a-half hour trip.

10.3.45

Ops Buer. Went deaf on the way back and have been told I will be u/s for flying for three days.

17.3.45

Bombed factory at Gneisenau near Dartmund.

19.3.45

Ops Gelsenkirchen. Skirted Dusseldorf and Essen and came in for a heavy pasting from all the guns there. The target was the old Benzole plant which was still half intact, and still is, as not a bomb landed on it. Some of the 149 Squadron Lancasters had a pretty thin time of it, and a bomb aimer was hit through the head on the run up and pegged out on the way back.

21.3.45

Ops Munster. Missed the aiming point again and three kites from 149 Squadron shot down.

22.3.45
Bocholt, a small town, came in for the next wallop from about 100 of us. We were in one of the first V's to bomb and I saw them burst smack into the centre of the town. Ten minutes later the pall of smoke from Bocholt reached up to 15,000 ft. On the way back noticed a smoke screen stretching from Arnhem to Duisburg – a large scale ground attack must be pending.

18.4.45
Set out for Heligoland. Almost 1,000 kites on this trip. This island guards the entrances to Bremen and Hamburg, key ports which the Germans are defending against attacks from British troops. Next to Heligoland is a smaller island almost entirely taken up by an aerodrome. This aerodrome was bombed first, followed by Heligoland. A huge column of smoke rose up, and inside the smoke a continuous series of angry red flashes showed where our bombs were exploding.

21.4.45
Bremen this afternoon, 149 Squadron leading the group, and our Wing Commander leading the squadron. We were flying to starboard of the Wing Commander. Some very accurate flak over Wilhelmshaven. Bombed in a small hail of flak.
(Note: I later heard that as our bombs fell on the east bank of the Weser the 52nd Division crossed the river.)

1.5.45
Holland from Rotterdam northward is still occupied, and to hold up our advance the Jerries have flooded half the country, with the result that the large towns are packed full of homeless and hungry Dutch people.

By some special arrangement we are being allowed to drop food on the towns without any opposition.

We set out at 11 am with 6,000 lbs of food for a place near

the Hague. Crossed the Dutch coast at low level near Overflakkee. The whole coastline and the banks of the rivers are pitted with defence posts and gun positions, though, true to their word, I never saw a German the whole time.

With Jerry under cover the population turned out in strength and waved at us – a heartening sight! Some of them were madly waving flags, all red, white and blue. One little man had an enormous flag in each hand and a terrific grin on his face. A woman was perched perilously on the roof of a house waving like mad and shouting something. I should think every person in the Hague turned out to cheer us.

Our dropping ground was in a sports field north of the town. With remarkable confidence in our aim the grandstand was packed and somebody looking very like the mayor was there in his robes of office.

Came back at nought feet across the sea, very pleased with ourselves.

7.5.45
Went to a village east of the Hague for another drop.

8.5.45
VE Day.

21.5.45
Flew to the aerodrome at Juvincourt this afternoon to pick up some of our boys – ex POWs. The weather was pretty duff and we stood in the rain with our 24 men waiting for take off, but the weather grew worse.

22.5.45
The weather cleared and we took off in the morning. One army lad was with me in the bombing compartment and when I pointed out the white cliffs of Dover he nearly jumped out of the kite in his excitement. He had been a prisoner for four years.

23.5.45

The crew was split up today. Bill and Pappy won't be flying with us anymore as they will be going home soon. Butch and Ken are joining another crew and the rest of us are spares.

*

Anyone reading these notes will be struck by the fact that not once during my time in Lancasters do I record mechanical, electrical or hydraulic faults, whereas these were common in Stirlings. Not only was the Lancaster more reliable, but she also had a higher ceiling, was faster and carried a heavier bomb load. Without doubt she was the queen of bombers.

Something which is not apparent in these notes, however, is the work done by the ground crews. Without fail they were magnificent, often working on aircraft in very windy and freezing conditions.

On 24.5.45 I received this letter from Cliff:

Dear Spud,
After many adventures, from the Polish border through Czech Sudentenland and Western Germany, I was released by men of Patten's army. In consequence of my condition being somewhat low I have since toured most Continental and British hospitals, growing stronger all the time and am now awaiting clearance. Two days ago I slipped from a US Field Hospital, went to Swindon and tried to get a train to Maidenhead, but owing to the lateness of the hour I could not make it. The treatment here leaves nothing to be desired but I am becoming impatient. Although I feel quite well I must wait until the RAF are satisfied that I am well. Yours etc.
Cliff.

Not long after receiving this letter from Cliff he managed to visit Maidenhead and I had a long chat with him about his experiences. He himself escaped a number of times, but was recaptured each time until the final escape mentioned in his letter. Cliff was tall and had very distinctive features, and it would have been very difficult for him to hide in a crowd. But it was while in prison that this particular talent came to the fore – given the right materials he could copy signatures, official forms, rubber stamps, passes etc., and armed with these a number of fellow prisoners did manage to escape. He was awarded an MBE some months after as a reward for these services. And so how exactly did he get the materials he needed while in prison? The prisoners used to get Red Cross parcels from time to time and these contained certain items greatly desired by the German guards. Once they had accepted such a gift it was possible to blackmail them into getting some of the materials you needed – even down to photographs of the right size for passes for those prisoners who didn't already have them. The fact was that the guards were under strict orders not to fraternise in any way with the prisoners.

All my RAF friends disappeared without trace within a year or two after we were demobbed. Cliff, I know, went to South Africa where he started up an advertising business; Shorty became a Draughtsman in Canada and Len went back to his old job in London, while Fred returned to the shoe industry in Northampton. But we were all too busy raising a family and earning a living to keep in touch.

In June '45 I joined up with a new crew and we flew on a few Reviews (i.e. taking aerial photographs for map-making purposes). The Russians fired at us one day when we got too close on their territory.

*

5.9.45
Up at 2 this morning for a Review. After a lot of fooling around took off about 7.30 and set course for Norway. Pretty chilly, about minus 25 degrees.

Coming back we dropped down and skirted the coast from Oslo to Stavanger before returning. Landed at 5pm.

(In January '46 we did odd flights, firing at smoke floats in the Wash: cross-countries, etc.)

16.8.45
In the early hours, woke up to find myself on the floor by my side of the bed in a cold sweat. I had had a nightmare in which my clothes were on fire and I was baling out of a burning aircraft. This woke up Marguerite who said, "You OK, Spud?" and I replied, "Yes, thanks."

And she said, "Stop mucking about then and get back into bed."
(Note: I stopped having these dreams a short time later and that was the only counselling I ever received.)

12.9.45
I have recently begun to think seriously about what will happen when I get to Civvy Street. Today I had an interview with Horton Giddy in Maidenhead. He gave me one of his frosty smiles and told me that he would be delighted to have me back. On the subject of wages he was quite definite. "Ten shillings a week, dear boy, and not a penny more." I thanked him for his kind offer and said that regretfully I would have to turn it down as I couldn't live on those wages. A pretty young woman sat at my old desk and gave me a sweet smile as I left.

On the way back to Methwold I was thinking about this situation when suddenly, out of the blue, I could see a solution. Andrew used to work for the Civil Service and he had told me what good employers they were. So I thought I would try and copy him.

13.9.45

Went to see the Education Officer, F/Lt Hollis, and asked him three questions:-
(1) Would I qualify for the Civil Service Reconstruction Exam?
(2) Could he supply me with exam papers etc?
(3) Could he find out for me whether the RAF would keep me on till I started work?

25.9.45

F/Lt Hollis asked to see me today.
(1) I could take the Reconstruction Exam.
(2) He could supply me with the necessary exam papers.
(3) The RAF would keep me on till I got fixed up.

This was a big relief and could be the answer to my problem. Made up my mind to swot like hell in the meantime.

13.10.45

Marguerite drank a lot of castor oil.

14.10.45

1 a.m. of a chilly clear morning. Marguerite was getting some pretty bad pains and I nipped off on the bike, banged as hard as I could on Pincott (taxi driver's) door. To Thetford at a snail's pace, with Marguerite's pains getting worse and the car running into odd patches of mist. Arrived at Nursing Home 2 a.m., taxi cleared off and I was kicked out by the Matron. Nothing for it but to walk back to the Shack, 15 miles and pitch dark. Once I heard a piercing scream – rustling, then silence. Kept thinking of Marguerite and imagining the worst.

Slept about two hours at the Shack and then set off for Thetford once more on the motorbike. Got a bed in the Anglo-American Club at the Bell Hotel and went to see Marguerite at 7 p.m. She was in bed, quite perky. In the next room was Christopher John who looked rather like a frog. The Matron says he looks like me.

8.1.46
Had a hilarious time at the flat in Clapham over Christmas.

Flew every day the last four days. First time across country – Isle of Man, Wales and back. Lovely day, could see the Welsh mountains delicately outlined in blue some 200 miles away. The next day we did some practice bombing, and the next some low flying over the Wash, firing at smoke floats. Today we took two WAAFs and three airmen on a Baideker – Dunkirk, Antwerp, Aachen, Duren, Cologne and then around Happy Valley. The debris in most towns had not yet been cleared away.

15.3.46
Bought a 1931 Austin 7 from a man in Brandon. After ten minutes tuition I drove off, but had forgotten to ask how to reverse!

April '46
The Squadron moved to Tuddenham and we found digs with Mrs Stewart, next door to the Comet Cinema in Mildenhall. It broke our hearts to leave the good old Shack.

August '46
Took the CS Exam in Cambridge. Was asked some questions of the type I had been give to study and others which I had never come across before. Felt a bit doubtful about the result.

September '46
Johnny came to see us – he is on his demob leave.

25.10.46
Today the sky was completely overcast over base as we took off in V Victor for some H/L Bombing. I had been told this was to be my last flight. Ten minutes later we burst through the cloud into dazzling sunshine and by the time we were over

the Wash we were at 20,000 ft and heading for the Lincolnshire coast. Our target, a coaster stranded on a sandbank, was clearly visible ahead. For the last time went into the familiar patter – "Left a bit Skipper, steady, steady, right a bit, steady, bombs gone." Our load was 8 x 250 lb HE and I watched them go down in a cluster until they disappeared from view. One hit the ship amidships and the rest churned up the water close by. We lost height and circled. This indestructible ship was still there but split in two, her funnel, masts and superstructure still showing clearly above the water, and all that my bombs had done was to drive her more firmly into the sand. "You haven't lost your grip then, you old bastard," said the pilot, which I took to be a compliment. Made my final checks that all the bombs had gone, etc., and we headed back towards Tuddenham.

18.11.46

Our 2nd Wedding Anniversary.

Mrs Stewart announced that she was pregnant by a Scottish LAC stationed at Tuddenham, and a brown envelope arrived with the results of the CS Exam. I have passed, but with rather poor marks, and have been offered Inland Revenue, Prison Service or Ministry of Labour.

Celebrated tonight with a pint of beer each.

28.11.46

Kay says she can offer us accommodation. I hope we will not inconvenience her too long. With a bit of luck I will get a Council House.

16.1.47

I was demobbed at Warton near Blackpool, when I was issued with an overcoat, flannels, sports coat and a pair of shoes.

*

Many years later I wrote this in my diary:

18.7.91
On the way back to Maidenhead with Aunt Kay we went to see if the Shack was still there in Brookville, but found that everything had changed.

The Shack has gone and has been replaced by a bungalow. The Post Office is now a private house, as is the Cock Public House, and Methwold aerodrome is now turned over to agriculture.

It is as if we had dreamed it all.